THIS BOOK BELONG TO:

WEB:

USER:

PASSWORD:

QUESTION:

NOTE:

WEB:

USER:

PASSWORD:

QUESTION:

NOTE:

WEB:

USER:

PASSWORD:

QUESTION:

NOTE:

WEB:

USER:

PASSWORD:

QUESTION:

NOTE:

WEB:

USER:

PASSWORD:

QUESTION:

NOTE:

WEB:

USER:

PASSWORD:

QUESTION:

NOTE:

WEB:

USER:

PASSWORD:

QUESTION:

NOTE:

WEB:

USER:

PASSWORD:

QUESTION:

NOTE:

WEB:

USER:

PASSWORD:

QUESTION:

NOTE:

WEB:

USER:

PASSWORD:

QUESTION:

NOTE:

WEB:

USER:

PASSWORD:

QUESTION:

NOTE:

WEB:

USER:

PASSWORD:

QUESTION:

NOTE:

WEB:

USER:

PASSWORD:

QUESTION:

NOTE:

WEB:

USER:

PASSWORD:

QUESTION:

NOTE:

WEB:

USER:

PASSWORD:

QUESTION:

NOTE:

WEB:

USER:

PASSWORD:

QUESTION:

NOTE:

WEB:

USER:

PASSWORD:

QUESTION:

NOTE:

WEB:

USER:

PASSWORD:

QUESTION:

NOTE:

WEB:

USER:

PASSWORD:

QUESTION:

NOTE:

WEB:

USER:

PASSWORD:

QUESTION:

NOTE:

WEB:

USER:

PASSWORD:

QUESTION:

NOTE:

WEB:

USER:

PASSWORD:

QUESTION:

NOTE:

WEB:

USER:

PASSWORD:

QUESTION:

NOTE:

WEB:

USER:

PASSWORD:

QUESTION:

NOTE:

WEB:

USER:

PASSWORD:

QUESTION:

NOTE:

WEB:

USER:

PASSWORD:

QUESTION:

NOTE:

WEB:

USER:

PASSWORD:

QUESTION:

NOTE:

WEB:

USER:

PASSWORD:

QUESTION:

NOTE:

WEB:

USER:

PASSWORD:

QUESTION:

NOTE:

WEB:

USER:

PASSWORD:

QUESTION:

NOTE:

WEB:

USER:

PASSWORD:

QUESTION:

NOTE:

WEB:

USER:

PASSWORD:

QUESTION:

NOTE:

WEB:

USER:

PASSWORD:

QUESTION:

NOTE:

WEB:

USER:

PASSWORD:

QUESTION:

NOTE:

WEB:

USER:

PASSWORD:

QUESTION:

NOTE:

WEB:

USER:

PASSWORD:

QUESTION:

NOTE:

WEB:

USER:

PASSWORD:

QUESTION:

NOTE:

WEB:

USER:

PASSWORD:

QUESTION:

NOTE:

WEB:

USER:

PASSWORD:

QUESTION:

NOTE:

WEB:

USER:

PASSWORD:

QUESTION:

NOTE:

WEB:

USER:

PASSWORD:

QUESTION:

NOTE:

WEB:

USER:

PASSWORD:

QUESTION:

NOTE:

WEB:

USER:

PASSWORD:

QUESTION:

NOTE:

WEB:

USER:

PASSWORD:

QUESTION:

NOTE:

WEB:

USER:

PASSWORD:

QUESTION:

NOTE:

WEB:

USER:

PASSWORD:

QUESTION:

NOTE:

WEB:

USER:

PASSWORD:

QUESTION:

NOTE:

WEB:

USER:

PASSWORD:

QUESTION:

NOTE:

WEB:

USER:

PASSWORD:

QUESTION:

NOTE:

WEB:

USER:

PASSWORD:

QUESTION:

NOTE:

WEB:

USER:

PASSWORD:

QUESTION:

NOTE:

WEB:

USER:

PASSWORD:

QUESTION:

NOTE:

WEB:

USER:

PASSWORD:

QUESTION:

NOTE:

WEB:

USER:

PASSWORD:

QUESTION:

NOTE:

WEB:

USER:

PASSWORD:

QUESTION:

NOTE:

WEB:

USER:

PASSWORD:

QUESTION:

NOTE:

WEB:

USER:

PASSWORD:

QUESTION:

NOTE:

WEB:

USER:

PASSWORD:

QUESTION:

NOTE:

WEB:

USER:

PASSWORD:

QUESTION:

NOTE:

WEB:

USER:

PASSWORD:

QUESTION:

NOTE:

WEB:

USER:

PASSWORD:

QUESTION:

NOTE:

WEB:

USER:

PASSWORD:

QUESTION:

NOTE:

WEB:

USER:

PASSWORD:

QUESTION:

NOTE:

WEB:

USER:

PASSWORD:

QUESTION:

NOTE:

WEB:

USER:

PASSWORD:

QUESTION:

NOTE:

WEB:

USER:

PASSWORD:

QUESTION:

NOTE:

WEB:

USER:

PASSWORD:

QUESTION:

NOTE:

WEB:

USER:

PASSWORD:

QUESTION:

NOTE:

WEB:

USER:

PASSWORD:

QUESTION:

NOTE:

WEB:

USER:

PASSWORD:

QUESTION:

NOTE:

WEB:

USER:

PASSWORD:

QUESTION:

NOTE:

WEB:

USER:

PASSWORD:

QUESTION:

NOTE:

WEB:

USER:

PASSWORD:

QUESTION:

NOTE:

WEB:

USER:

PASSWORD:

QUESTION:

NOTE:

WEB:

USER:

PASSWORD:

QUESTION:

NOTE:

WEB:

USER:

PASSWORD:

QUESTION:

NOTE:

WEB: _____

USER: _____

PASSWORD: _____

QUESTION: _____

NOTE: _____

WEB: _____

USER: _____

PASSWORD: _____

QUESTION: _____

NOTE: _____

WEB: _____

USER: _____

PASSWORD: _____

QUESTION: _____

NOTE: _____

WEB: _____

USER: _____

PASSWORD: _____

QUESTION: _____

NOTE: _____

WEB:

USER:

PASSWORD:

QUESTION:

NOTE:

WEB:

USER:

PASSWORD:

QUESTION:

NOTE:

WEB:

USER:

PASSWORD:

QUESTION:

NOTE:

WEB:

USER:

PASSWORD:

QUESTION:

NOTE:

WEB:

USER:

PASSWORD:

QUESTION:

NOTE:

WEB:

USER:

PASSWORD:

QUESTION:

NOTE:

WEB:

USER:

PASSWORD:

QUESTION:

NOTE:

WEB:

USER:

PASSWORD:

QUESTION:

NOTE:

WEB:

USER:

PASSWORD:

QUESTION:

NOTE:

WEB:

USER:

PASSWORD:

QUESTION:

NOTE:

WEB:

USER:

PASSWORD:

QUESTION:

NOTE:

WEB:

USER:

PASSWORD:

QUESTION:

NOTE:

WEB:

USER:

PASSWORD:

QUESTION:

NOTE:

WEB:

USER:

PASSWORD:

QUESTION:

NOTE:

WEB:

USER:

PASSWORD:

QUESTION:

NOTE:

WEB:

USER:

PASSWORD:

QUESTION:

NOTE:

WEB:

USER:

PASSWORD:

QUESTION:

NOTE:

WEB:

USER:

PASSWORD:

QUESTION:

NOTE:

WEB:

USER:

PASSWORD:

QUESTION:

NOTE:

WEB:

USER:

PASSWORD:

QUESTION:

NOTE:

WEB:

USER:

PASSWORD:

QUESTION:

NOTE:

WEB:

USER:

PASSWORD:

QUESTION:

NOTE:

WEB:

USER:

PASSWORD:

QUESTION:

NOTE:

WEB:

USER:

PASSWORD:

QUESTION:

NOTE:

WEB:

USER:

PASSWORD:

QUESTION:

NOTE:

WEB:

USER:

PASSWORD:

QUESTION:

NOTE:

WEB:

USER:

PASSWORD:

QUESTION:

NOTE:

WEB:

USER:

PASSWORD:

QUESTION:

NOTE:

WEB:

USER:

PASSWORD:

QUESTION:

NOTE:

WEB:

USER:

PASSWORD:

QUESTION:

NOTE:

WEB:

USER:

PASSWORD:

QUESTION:

NOTE:

WEB:

USER:

PASSWORD:

QUESTION:

NOTE:

WEB:

USER:

PASSWORD:

QUESTION:

NOTE:

WEB:

USER:

PASSWORD:

QUESTION:

NOTE:

WEB:

USER:

PASSWORD:

QUESTION:

NOTE:

WEB:

USER:

PASSWORD:

QUESTION:

NOTE:

WEB:

USER:

PASSWORD:

QUESTION:

NOTE:

WEB:

USER:

PASSWORD:

QUESTION:

NOTE:

WEB:

USER:

PASSWORD:

QUESTION:

NOTE:

WEB:

USER:

PASSWORD:

QUESTION:

NOTE:

WEB:

USER:

PASSWORD:

QUESTION:

NOTE:

WEB:

USER:

PASSWORD:

QUESTION:

NOTE:

WEB:

USER:

PASSWORD:

QUESTION:

NOTE:

WEB:

USER:

PASSWORD:

QUESTION:

NOTE:

WEB:

USER:

PASSWORD:

QUESTION:

NOTE:

WEB:

USER:

PASSWORD:

QUESTION:

NOTE:

WEB:

USER:

PASSWORD:

QUESTION:

NOTE:

WEB:

USER:

PASSWORD:

QUESTION:

NOTE:

WEB:

USER:

PASSWORD:

QUESTION:

NOTE:

WEB:

USER:

PASSWORD:

QUESTION:

NOTE:

WEB:

USER:

PASSWORD:

QUESTION:

NOTE:

WEB:

USER:

PASSWORD:

QUESTION:

NOTE:

WEB:

USER:

PASSWORD:

QUESTION:

NOTE:

WEB:

USER:

PASSWORD:

QUESTION:

NOTE:

WEB:

USER:

PASSWORD:

QUESTION:

NOTE:

WEB:

USER:

PASSWORD:

QUESTION:

NOTE:

WEB:

USER:

PASSWORD:

QUESTION:

NOTE:

WEB:

USER:

PASSWORD:

QUESTION:

NOTE:

WEB:

USER:

PASSWORD:

QUESTION:

NOTE:

WEB:

USER:

PASSWORD:

QUESTION:

NOTE:

WEB:

USER:

PASSWORD:

QUESTION:

NOTE:

WEB:

USER:

PASSWORD:

QUESTION:

NOTE:

WEB:

USER:

PASSWORD:

QUESTION:

NOTE:

WEB:

USER:

PASSWORD:

QUESTION:

NOTE:

WEB:

USER:

PASSWORD:

QUESTION:

NOTE:

WEB:

USER:

PASSWORD:

QUESTION:

NOTE:

WEB:

USER:

PASSWORD:

QUESTION:

NOTE:

WEB:

USER:

PASSWORD:

QUESTION:

NOTE:

WEB:

USER:

PASSWORD:

QUESTION:

NOTE:

WEB:

USER:

PASSWORD:

QUESTION:

NOTE:

WEB:

USER:

PASSWORD:

QUESTION:

NOTE:

WEB:

USER:

PASSWORD:

QUESTION:

NOTE:

WEB:

USER:

PASSWORD:

QUESTION:

NOTE:

WEB:

USER:

PASSWORD:

QUESTION:

NOTE:

WEB:

USER:

PASSWORD:

QUESTION:

NOTE:

WEB:

USER:

PASSWORD:

QUESTION:

NOTE:

WEB:

USER:

PASSWORD:

QUESTION:

NOTE:

WEB:

USER:

PASSWORD:

QUESTION:

NOTE:

WEB:

USER:

PASSWORD:

QUESTION:

NOTE:

WEB:

USER:

PASSWORD:

QUESTION:

NOTE:

WEB:

USER:

PASSWORD:

QUESTION:

NOTE:

WEB:

USER:

PASSWORD:

QUESTION:

NOTE:

WEB:

USER:

PASSWORD:

QUESTION:

NOTE:

WEB:

USER:

PASSWORD:

QUESTION:

NOTE:

WEB:

USER:

PASSWORD:

QUESTION:

NOTE:

WEB:

USER:

PASSWORD:

QUESTION:

NOTE:

WEB:

USER:

PASSWORD:

QUESTION:

NOTE:

WEB:

USER:

PASSWORD:

QUESTION:

NOTE:

WEB:

USER:

PASSWORD:

QUESTION:

NOTE:

WEB:

USER:

PASSWORD:

QUESTION:

NOTE:

WEB:

USER:

PASSWORD:

QUESTION:

NOTE:

WEB:

USER:

PASSWORD:

QUESTION:

NOTE:

WEB: _____

USER: _____

PASSWORD: _____

QUESTION: _____

NOTE: _____

WEB: _____

USER: _____

PASSWORD: _____

QUESTION: _____

NOTE: _____

WEB: _____

USER: _____

PASSWORD: _____

QUESTION: _____

NOTE: _____

WEB: _____

USER: _____

PASSWORD: _____

QUESTION: _____

NOTE: _____

WEB:

USER:

PASSWORD:

QUESTION:

NOTE:

WEB:

USER:

PASSWORD:

QUESTION:

NOTE:

WEB:

USER:

PASSWORD:

QUESTION:

NOTE:

WEB:

USER:

PASSWORD:

QUESTION:

NOTE:

WEB:

USER:

PASSWORD:

QUESTION:

NOTE:

WEB:

USER:

PASSWORD:

QUESTION:

NOTE:

WEB:

USER:

PASSWORD:

QUESTION:

NOTE:

WEB:

USER:

PASSWORD:

QUESTION:

NOTE:

WEB:

USER:

PASSWORD:

QUESTION:

NOTE:

WEB:

USER:

PASSWORD:

QUESTION:

NOTE:

WEB:

USER:

PASSWORD:

QUESTION:

NOTE:

WEB:

USER:

PASSWORD:

QUESTION:

NOTE:

WEB:

USER:

PASSWORD:

QUESTION:

NOTE:

WEB:

USER:

PASSWORD:

QUESTION:

NOTE:

WEB:

USER:

PASSWORD:

QUESTION:

NOTE:

WEB:

USER:

PASSWORD:

QUESTION:

NOTE:

WEB:

USER:

PASSWORD:

QUESTION:

NOTE:

WEB:

USER:

PASSWORD:

QUESTION:

NOTE:

WEB:

USER:

PASSWORD:

QUESTION:

NOTE:

WEB:

USER:

PASSWORD:

QUESTION:

NOTE:

WEB:

USER:

PASSWORD:

QUESTION:

NOTE:

WEB:

USER:

PASSWORD:

QUESTION:

NOTE:

WEB:

USER:

PASSWORD:

QUESTION:

NOTE:

WEB:

USER:

PASSWORD:

QUESTION:

NOTE:

WEB:

USER:

PASSWORD:

QUESTION:

NOTE:

WEB:

USER:

PASSWORD:

QUESTION:

NOTE:

WEB:

USER:

PASSWORD:

QUESTION:

NOTE:

WEB:

USER:

PASSWORD:

QUESTION:

NOTE:

WEB:

USER:

PASSWORD:

QUESTION:

NOTE:

WEB:

USER:

PASSWORD:

QUESTION:

NOTE:

WEB:

USER:

PASSWORD:

QUESTION:

NOTE:

WEB:

USER:

PASSWORD:

QUESTION:

NOTE:

WEB:

USER:

PASSWORD:

QUESTION:

NOTE:

WEB:

USER:

PASSWORD:

QUESTION:

NOTE:

WEB:

USER:

PASSWORD:

QUESTION:

NOTE:

WEB:

USER:

PASSWORD:

QUESTION:

NOTE:

WEB:

USER:

PASSWORD:

QUESTION:

NOTE:

WEB:

USER:

PASSWORD:

QUESTION:

NOTE:

WEB:

USER:

PASSWORD:

QUESTION:

NOTE:

WEB:

USER:

PASSWORD:

QUESTION:

NOTE:

WEB:

USER:

PASSWORD:

QUESTION:

NOTE:

WEB:

USER:

PASSWORD:

QUESTION:

NOTE:

WEB:

USER:

PASSWORD:

QUESTION:

NOTE:

WEB:

USER:

PASSWORD:

QUESTION:

NOTE:

WEB:

USER:

PASSWORD:

QUESTION:

NOTE:

WEB:

USER:

PASSWORD:

QUESTION:

NOTE:

WEB:

USER:

PASSWORD:

QUESTION:

NOTE:

WEB:

USER:

PASSWORD:

QUESTION:

NOTE:

WEB:

USER:

PASSWORD:

QUESTION:

NOTE:

WEB:

USER:

PASSWORD:

QUESTION:

NOTE:

WEB:

USER:

PASSWORD:

QUESTION:

NOTE:

WEB:

USER:

PASSWORD:

QUESTION:

NOTE:

WEB:

USER:

PASSWORD:

QUESTION:

NOTE:

WEB:

USER:

PASSWORD:

QUESTION:

NOTE:

WEB:

USER:

PASSWORD:

QUESTION:

NOTE:

WEB:

USER:

PASSWORD:

QUESTION:

NOTE:

WEB:

USER:

PASSWORD:

QUESTION:

NOTE:

WEB:

USER:

PASSWORD:

QUESTION:

NOTE:

WEB:

USER:

PASSWORD:

QUESTION:

NOTE:

WEB:

USER:

PASSWORD:

QUESTION:

NOTE:

WEB:

USER:

PASSWORD:

QUESTION:

NOTE:

WEB:

USER:

PASSWORD:

QUESTION:

NOTE:

WEB:

USER:

PASSWORD:

QUESTION:

NOTE:

WEB:

USER:

PASSWORD:

QUESTION:

NOTE:

WEB:

USER:

PASSWORD:

QUESTION:

NOTE:

WEB:

USER:

PASSWORD:

QUESTION:

NOTE:

WEB:

USER:

PASSWORD:

QUESTION:

NOTE:

WEB:

USER:

PASSWORD:

QUESTION:

NOTE:

WEB:

USER:

PASSWORD:

QUESTION:

NOTE:

WEB:

USER:

PASSWORD:

QUESTION:

NOTE:

WEB:

USER:

PASSWORD:

QUESTION:

NOTE:

WEB:

USER:

PASSWORD:

QUESTION:

NOTE:

WEB:

USER:

PASSWORD:

QUESTION:

NOTE:

WEB:

USER:

PASSWORD:

QUESTION:

NOTE:

WEB:

USER:

PASSWORD:

QUESTION:

NOTE:

WEB:

USER:

PASSWORD:

QUESTION:

NOTE:

WEB:

USER:

PASSWORD:

QUESTION:

NOTE:

WEB:

USER:

PASSWORD:

QUESTION:

NOTE:

WEB:

USER:

PASSWORD:

QUESTION:

NOTE:

WEB:

USER:

PASSWORD:

QUESTION:

NOTE:

WEB:

USER:

PASSWORD:

QUESTION:

NOTE:

WEB:

USER:

PASSWORD:

QUESTION:

NOTE:

WEB:

USER:

PASSWORD:

QUESTION:

NOTE:

WEB:

USER:

PASSWORD:

QUESTION:

NOTE:

WEB:

USER:

PASSWORD:

QUESTION:

NOTE:

WEB:

USER:

PASSWORD:

QUESTION:

NOTE:

WEB:

USER:

PASSWORD:

QUESTION:

NOTE:

WEB:

USER:

PASSWORD:

QUESTION:

NOTE:

WEB:

USER:

PASSWORD:

QUESTION:

NOTE:

WEB:

USER:

PASSWORD:

QUESTION:

NOTE:

WEB:

USER:

PASSWORD:

QUESTION:

NOTE:

WEB:

USER:

PASSWORD:

QUESTION:

NOTE:

WEB:

USER:

PASSWORD:

QUESTION:

NOTE:

WEB:

USER:

PASSWORD:

QUESTION:

NOTE:

WEB:

USER:

PASSWORD:

QUESTION:

NOTE:

WEB:

USER:

PASSWORD:

QUESTION:

NOTE:

WEB:

USER:

PASSWORD:

QUESTION:

NOTE:

WEB:

USER:

PASSWORD:

QUESTION:

NOTE:

WEB:

USER:

PASSWORD:

QUESTION:

NOTE:

WEB:

USER:

PASSWORD:

QUESTION:

NOTE:

WEB:

USER:

PASSWORD:

QUESTION:

NOTE:

WEB:

USER:

PASSWORD:

QUESTION:

NOTE:

WEB:

USER:

PASSWORD:

QUESTION:

NOTE:

WEB:

USER:

PASSWORD:

QUESTION:

NOTE:

WEB:

USER:

PASSWORD:

QUESTION:

NOTE:

WEB:

USER:

PASSWORD:

QUESTION:

NOTE:

WEB:

USER:

PASSWORD:

QUESTION:

NOTE:

WEB:

USER:

PASSWORD:

QUESTION:

NOTE:

WEB:

USER:

PASSWORD:

QUESTION:

NOTE:

WEB:

USER:

PASSWORD:

QUESTION:

NOTE:

WEB:

USER:

PASSWORD:

QUESTION:

NOTE:

WEB:

USER:

PASSWORD:

QUESTION:

NOTE:

WEB:

USER:

PASSWORD:

QUESTION:

NOTE:

WEB:

USER:

PASSWORD:

QUESTION:

NOTE:

WEB:

USER:

PASSWORD:

QUESTION:

NOTE:

WEB:

USER:

PASSWORD:

QUESTION:

NOTE:

WEB:

USER:

PASSWORD:

QUESTION:

NOTE:

WEB:

USER:

PASSWORD:

QUESTION:

NOTE:

WEB:

USER:

PASSWORD:

QUESTION:

NOTE:

WEB:

USER:

PASSWORD:

QUESTION:

NOTE:

WEB:

USER:

PASSWORD:

QUESTION:

NOTE:

WEB:

USER:

PASSWORD:

QUESTION:

NOTE:

WEB:

USER:

PASSWORD:

QUESTION:

NOTE:

WEB:

USER:

PASSWORD:

QUESTION:

NOTE:

WEB:

USER:

PASSWORD:

QUESTION:

NOTE:

WEB:

USER:

PASSWORD:

QUESTION:

NOTE:

WEB:

USER:

PASSWORD:

QUESTION:

NOTE:

WEB:

USER:

PASSWORD:

QUESTION:

NOTE:

WEB:

USER:

PASSWORD:

QUESTION:

NOTE:

WEB:

USER:

PASSWORD:

QUESTION:

NOTE:

WEB:

USER:

PASSWORD:

QUESTION:

NOTE:

WEB:

USER:

PASSWORD:

QUESTION:

NOTE:

WEB:

USER:

PASSWORD:

QUESTION:

NOTE:

WEB:

USER:

PASSWORD:

QUESTION:

NOTE:

WEB:

USER:

PASSWORD:

QUESTION:

NOTE:

WEB:

USER:

PASSWORD:

QUESTION:

NOTE:

WEB:

USER:

PASSWORD:

QUESTION:

NOTE:

WEB:

USER:

PASSWORD:

QUESTION:

NOTE:

WEB:

USER:

PASSWORD:

QUESTION:

NOTE:

WEB:

USER:

PASSWORD:

QUESTION:

NOTE:

WEB:

USER:

PASSWORD:

QUESTION:

NOTE:

WEB:

USER:

PASSWORD:

QUESTION:

NOTE:

WEB:

USER:

PASSWORD:

QUESTION:

NOTE:

WEB:

USER:

PASSWORD:

QUESTION:

NOTE:

WEB:

USER:

PASSWORD:

QUESTION:

NOTE:

WEB:

USER:

PASSWORD:

QUESTION:

NOTE:

WEB:

USER:

PASSWORD:

QUESTION:

NOTE:

WEB:

USER:

PASSWORD:

QUESTION:

NOTE:

WEB:

USER:

PASSWORD:

QUESTION:

NOTE:

WEB:

USER:

PASSWORD:

QUESTION:

NOTE:

WEB:

USER:

PASSWORD:

QUESTION:

NOTE:

WEB:

USER:

PASSWORD:

QUESTION:

NOTE:

WEB:

USER:

PASSWORD:

QUESTION:

NOTE:

WEB:

USER:

PASSWORD:

QUESTION:

NOTE:

WEB:

USER:

PASSWORD:

QUESTION:

NOTE:

WEB:

USER:

PASSWORD:

QUESTION:

NOTE:

WEB:

USER:

PASSWORD:

QUESTION:

NOTE:

WEB:

USER:

PASSWORD:

QUESTION:

NOTE:

WEB:

USER:

PASSWORD:

QUESTION:

NOTE:

WEB:

USER:

PASSWORD:

QUESTION:

NOTE:

WEB:

USER:

PASSWORD:

QUESTION:

NOTE:

WEB:

USER:

PASSWORD:

QUESTION:

NOTE:

WEB:

USER:

PASSWORD:

QUESTION:

NOTE:

WEB:

USER:

PASSWORD:

QUESTION:

NOTE:

WEB:

USER:

PASSWORD:

QUESTION:

NOTE:

WEB:

USER:

PASSWORD:

QUESTION:

NOTE:

WEB:

USER:

PASSWORD:

QUESTION:

NOTE:

WEB:

USER:

PASSWORD:

QUESTION:

NOTE:

WEB:

USER:

PASSWORD:

QUESTION:

NOTE:

WEB:

USER:

PASSWORD:

QUESTION:

NOTE:

WEB:

USER:

PASSWORD:

QUESTION:

NOTE:

WEB:

USER:

PASSWORD:

QUESTION:

NOTE:

WEB:

USER:

PASSWORD:

QUESTION:

NOTE:

WEB:

USER:

PASSWORD:

QUESTION:

NOTE:

WEB:

USER:

PASSWORD:

QUESTION:

NOTE:

WEB:

USER:

PASSWORD:

QUESTION:

NOTE:

WEB:

USER:

PASSWORD:

QUESTION:

NOTE:

WEB:

USER:

PASSWORD:

QUESTION:

NOTE:

WEB:

USER:

PASSWORD:

QUESTION:

NOTE:

WEB:

USER:

PASSWORD:

QUESTION:

NOTE:

WEB:

USER:

PASSWORD:

QUESTION:

NOTE:

WEB:

USER:

PASSWORD:

QUESTION:

NOTE:

WEB:

USER:

PASSWORD:

QUESTION:

NOTE:

WEB:

USER:

PASSWORD:

QUESTION:

NOTE:

WEB:

USER:

PASSWORD:

QUESTION:

NOTE:

WEB:

USER:

PASSWORD:

QUESTION:

NOTE:

WEB:

USER:

PASSWORD:

QUESTION:

NOTE:

WEB:

USER:

PASSWORD:

QUESTION:

NOTE:

WEB:

USER:

PASSWORD:

QUESTION:

NOTE:

WEB:

USER:

PASSWORD:

QUESTION:

NOTE:

WEB:

USER:

PASSWORD:

QUESTION:

NOTE:

WEB:

USER:

PASSWORD:

QUESTION:

NOTE:

WEB:

USER:

PASSWORD:

QUESTION:

NOTE:

WEB:

USER:

PASSWORD:

QUESTION:

NOTE:

WEB:

USER:

PASSWORD:

QUESTION:

NOTE:

WEB:

USER:

PASSWORD:

QUESTION:

NOTE:

WEB:

USER:

PASSWORD:

QUESTION:

NOTE:

WEB:

USER:

PASSWORD:

QUESTION:

NOTE:

WEB:

USER:

PASSWORD:

QUESTION:

NOTE:

WEB:

USER:

PASSWORD:

QUESTION:

NOTE:

WEB:

USER:

PASSWORD:

QUESTION:

NOTE:

WEB:

USER:

PASSWORD:

QUESTION:

NOTE:

WEB:

USER:

PASSWORD:

QUESTION:

NOTE:

WEB:

USER:

PASSWORD:

QUESTION:

NOTE:

WEB:

USER:

PASSWORD:

QUESTION:

NOTE:

WEB:

USER:

PASSWORD:

QUESTION:

NOTE:

WEB:

USER:

PASSWORD:

QUESTION:

NOTE:

WEB:

USER:

PASSWORD:

QUESTION:

NOTE:

WEB:

USER:

PASSWORD:

QUESTION:

NOTE:

WEB:

USER:

PASSWORD:

QUESTION:

NOTE:

WEB:

USER:

PASSWORD:

QUESTION:

NOTE:

WEB:

USER:

PASSWORD:

QUESTION:

NOTE:

WEB:

USER:

PASSWORD:

QUESTION:

NOTE:

WEB:

USER:

PASSWORD:

QUESTION:

NOTE:

WEB:

USER:

PASSWORD:

QUESTION:

NOTE:

WEB:

USER:

PASSWORD:

QUESTION:

NOTE:

WEB:

USER:

PASSWORD:

QUESTION:

NOTE:

WEB:

USER:

PASSWORD:

QUESTION:

NOTE:

WEB:

USER:

PASSWORD:

QUESTION:

NOTE:

WEB:

USER:

PASSWORD:

QUESTION:

NOTE:

WEB:

USER:

PASSWORD:

QUESTION:

NOTE:

WEB:

USER:

PASSWORD:

QUESTION:

NOTE:

WEB:

USER:

PASSWORD:

QUESTION:

NOTE:

WEB:

USER:

PASSWORD:

QUESTION:

NOTE:

WEB:

USER:

PASSWORD:

QUESTION:

NOTE:

WEB:

USER:

PASSWORD:

QUESTION:

NOTE:

WEB:

USER:

PASSWORD:

QUESTION:

NOTE:

WEB:

USER:

PASSWORD:

QUESTION:

NOTE:

WEB:

USER:

PASSWORD:

QUESTION:

NOTE:

WEB:

USER:

PASSWORD:

QUESTION:

NOTE:

WEB:

USER:

PASSWORD:

QUESTION:

NOTE:

WEB:

USER:

PASSWORD:

QUESTION:

NOTE:

WEB:

USER:

PASSWORD:

QUESTION:

NOTE:

WEB:

USER:

PASSWORD:

QUESTION:

NOTE:

WEB:

USER:

PASSWORD:

QUESTION:

NOTE:

WEB:

USER:

PASSWORD:

QUESTION:

NOTE:

WEB:

USER:

PASSWORD:

QUESTION:

NOTE:

WEB:

USER:

PASSWORD:

QUESTION:

NOTE:

WEB:

USER:

PASSWORD:

QUESTION:

NOTE:

WEB:

USER:

PASSWORD:

QUESTION:

NOTE:

WEB:

USER:

PASSWORD:

QUESTION:

NOTE:

WEB:

USER:

PASSWORD:

QUESTION:

NOTE:

WEB:

USER:

PASSWORD:

QUESTION:

NOTE:

WEB:

USER:

PASSWORD:

QUESTION:

NOTE:

WEB:

USER:

PASSWORD:

QUESTION:

NOTE:

WEB:

USER:

PASSWORD:

QUESTION:

NOTE:

WEB:

USER:

PASSWORD:

QUESTION:

NOTE:

WEB:

USER:

PASSWORD:

QUESTION:

NOTE:

WEB:

USER:

PASSWORD:

QUESTION:

NOTE:

WEB:

USER:

PASSWORD:

QUESTION:

NOTE:

WEB:

USER:

PASSWORD:

QUESTION:

NOTE:

WEB:

USER:

PASSWORD:

QUESTION:

NOTE:

WEB:

USER:

PASSWORD:

QUESTION:

NOTE:

WEB:

USER:

PASSWORD:

QUESTION:

NOTE:

WEB:

USER:

PASSWORD:

QUESTION:

NOTE:

WEB:

USER:

PASSWORD:

QUESTION:

NOTE:

WEB:

USER:

PASSWORD:

QUESTION:

NOTE:

WEB:

USER:

PASSWORD:

QUESTION:

NOTE:

WEB:

USER:

PASSWORD:

QUESTION:

NOTE:

WEB:

USER:

PASSWORD:

QUESTION:

NOTE:

WEB:

USER:

PASSWORD:

QUESTION:

NOTE:

WEB:

USER:

PASSWORD:

QUESTION:

NOTE:

WEB:

USER:

PASSWORD:

QUESTION:

NOTE:

WEB:

USER:

PASSWORD:

QUESTION:

NOTE:

WEB:

USER:

PASSWORD:

QUESTION:

NOTE:

WEB:

USER:

PASSWORD:

QUESTION:

NOTE:

WEB:

USER:

PASSWORD:

QUESTION:

NOTE:

WEB:

USER:

PASSWORD:

QUESTION:

NOTE:

WEB:

USER:

PASSWORD:

QUESTION:

NOTE:

WEB:

USER:

PASSWORD:

QUESTION:

NOTE:

WEB:

USER:

PASSWORD:

QUESTION:

NOTE:

WEB:

USER:

PASSWORD:

QUESTION:

NOTE:

WEB:

USER:

PASSWORD:

QUESTION:

NOTE:

WEB:

USER:

PASSWORD:

QUESTION:

NOTE:

WEB:

USER:

PASSWORD:

QUESTION:

NOTE:

WEB:

USER:

PASSWORD:

QUESTION:

NOTE:

WEB:

USER:

PASSWORD:

QUESTION:

NOTE:

WEB:

USER:

PASSWORD:

QUESTION:

NOTE:

WEB:

USER:

PASSWORD:

QUESTION:

NOTE:

WEB:

USER:

PASSWORD:

QUESTION:

NOTE:

WEB:

USER:

PASSWORD:

QUESTION:

NOTE:

WEB:

USER:

PASSWORD:

QUESTION:

NOTE:

WEB:

USER:

PASSWORD:

QUESTION:

NOTE:

WEB:

USER:

PASSWORD:

QUESTION:

NOTE:

WEB:

USER:

PASSWORD:

QUESTION:

NOTE:

WEB:

USER:

PASSWORD:

QUESTION:

NOTE:

WEB:

USER:

PASSWORD:

QUESTION:

NOTE:

WEB:

USER:

PASSWORD:

QUESTION:

NOTE:

WEB:

USER:

PASSWORD:

QUESTION:

NOTE:

WEB:

USER:

PASSWORD:

QUESTION:

NOTE:

WEB:

USER:

PASSWORD:

QUESTION:

NOTE:

WEB:

USER:

PASSWORD:

QUESTION:

NOTE:

WEB:

USER:

PASSWORD:

QUESTION:

NOTE:

WEB:

USER:

PASSWORD:

QUESTION:

NOTE:

WEB:

USER:

PASSWORD:

QUESTION:

NOTE:

WEB:

USER:

PASSWORD:

QUESTION:

NOTE:

WEB:

USER:

PASSWORD:

QUESTION:

NOTE:

WEB:

USER:

PASSWORD:

QUESTION:

NOTE:

WEB:

USER:

PASSWORD:

QUESTION:

NOTE:

WEB:

USER:

PASSWORD:

QUESTION:

NOTE:

www.ingramcontent.com/pod-product-compliance
Lightning Source LLC
Chambersburg PA
CBHW080538060326
40690CB00022B/5167